03963348

990064

D0347767

Really Wild
SHARKS

TAKE-OFF!

Claire Robinson

Heinemann
LIBRARY

First published in Great Britain by Heinemann Library
Halley Court, Jordan Hill, Oxford OX2 8EJ,
a division of Reed Educational and Professional Publishing Ltd.

OXFORD MELBOURNE AUCKLAND
IBADAN BLANTYRE JOHANNESBURG GABORONE
PORTSMOUTH NH (USA) CHICAGO

© Reed Educational and Professional Publishing Ltd 2000

The moral right of the proprietor has been asserted.

All rights reserved. No part of this publication may be reproduced, stored in a retrieval system,
or transmitted in any form or by any means, electronic, mechanical, photocopying, recording,
or otherwise without either the prior written permission of the Publishers or a licence permitting
restricted copying in the United Kingdom issued by the Copyright Licensing Agency Ltd,
90 Tottenham Court Road, London W1P 0LP.

Designed by Celia Floyd
Illustrations by Alan Fraser (Pennant Illustration) and Hardlines (map p.6)
Colour reproduction by Dot Gradations, UK.
Printed and bound in Hong Kong/China

04 03 02 01 00
10 9 8 7 6 5 4 3 2

ISBN 0 431 02893 1
This book is also available in hardback (ISBN 0 431 02888 5),

British Library Cataloguing in Publication Data

Robinson, Claire
Shark. – (Really wild) (Take-off!)
1. Sharks – Juvenile literature
I. Title
597.3

BRENT LIBRARY SERVICE	
03963348	
PETERS	28-Oct-02
£5.50	TOW

Look at the shark at the bottom of each page. Flick the pages and see what happens!

Acknowledgements

The Publishers would like to thank the following for permission to reproduce photographs:
Ardea London Ltd: p.16, Valerie Taylor pp.6, 20, Ian Gordon p.19; BBC Natural History Unit:
David Hall, pp.4 (right), 9, Dan Burton p.5 (left), Jeff Rotman pp.11, 21; Bruce Coleman
Limited: Franco Banfi p.4 (left), Michael Glover p.18; Oxford Scientific Films: Tom McHugh p.5
(left), G.I. Bernard p.17, David B. Fleetham pp. 7, 14, 23, Bruce Watkins p.10,
Richard Herrmann p.12, John Lidington p.13, Pam & Willy Kemp p.15, Tui de Roy p.22;
Wildlife Matters: p.8.

Cover photograph: The Stock Market/Amos Nachoum

Our thanks to Sue Graves for her advice and expertise in the preparation of this book.

Every effort has been made to contact copyright holders of any material reproduced in this
book. Any omissions will be rectified in subsequent printings if notice is given to the Publisher.

For more information about Heinemann Library books, or to order, please telephone
+44(0)1865 888066, or send a fax to +44(0)1865 314091. You can visit our website at
www.heinemann.co.uk

Contents

Some words are shown in bold, **like this**. You can find out what they mean by looking in the glossary.

Shark relatives

Sharks are fish. The whale shark is the biggest fish in the world. Some whale sharks are 12 metres (40 feet) long.

The whale shark is the biggest fish in the world.

The blue shark can travel thousands of kilometres in a year.

A black-tip reef shark gets its name from the black on its fins.

Some dogfish sharks are only 30 cms long.

Most sharks are less than 2 metres long. Dogfish sharks are small, some only 30 cms long. There are more than 250 different kinds of shark in the world. Let's find out how some of them live.

Where do sharks live?

Sharks can be found in seas all over the world. Reef sharks can be found near **coral** reefs in the Indian and Pacific oceans. They like to live in the warm, **shallow** seas near these reefs. They hunt for food at night.

coral reef

The reef shark likes to hunt at night.

Other sharks live in deeper parts of the oceans.
Blue sharks and white-tip sharks are found in
the Pacific, Indian and Atlantic Oceans.

How many white-tip sharks can you see in this picture?

Moving around

This shark sweeps its tail from side to side as it swims.

Sharks swim by sweeping their tails from side to side. The large side fins help them to swim upwards or dive down deep.

Sharks have to keep swimming or they will sink!

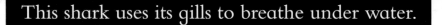

gill slit

This shark uses its gills to breathe under water.

Fish do not have to go to the **surface** to get air. They can breathe under water. They breathe in through their mouth and out through their **gills**. This shark has five gills on each side of its body.

Senses

Sharks have good eyesight. They see well in the dim, ocean light. Sharks do not have any eyelids. Eyelids keep our eyes moist, but because sharks live under the water, they don't need any. So you will never see a shark blink.

eye

Sharks do not need eyelids because they live under water.

Sharks have a strong sense of smell too. This blue shark can smell something to eat a long way away. She is hungry so she goes to find food.

This blue shark uses her strong sense of smell to find food.

Finding food

shoal of fish

This blue shark has found a **shoal** of fish to eat.

Sharks are hunters. They hunt for other fish. They also like to eat octopus and crabs. Bigger sharks eat turtles, dolphins, and sea-lions.

A shark can smell blood in the water from one kilometre away.

Some sharks find their food on the sea bed. The nurse shark is a lazy hunter. It catches slow-moving animals in **shallow** water.

This nurse shark feels in the sand for any animals hiding there.

Feeding

teeth

These teeth are good for catching fish.

This sand shark looks very fierce. It has many rows of sharp, pointed teeth. When the front ones break off, the teeth behind move forwards to take their place.

These reef sharks swim quickly to catch some food.

These reef sharks smelt food and rushed in to feed. Sharks have good hearing. They can hear the sound of a fish moving quickly or struggling on a fishing line from a long way away.

Baby sharks

Some sharks give birth to live young and others lay eggs. Baby dogfish sharks grow inside an egg case called a '**mermaid's purse**'. The mermaid's purse has long **tendrils** which wind around seaweed.

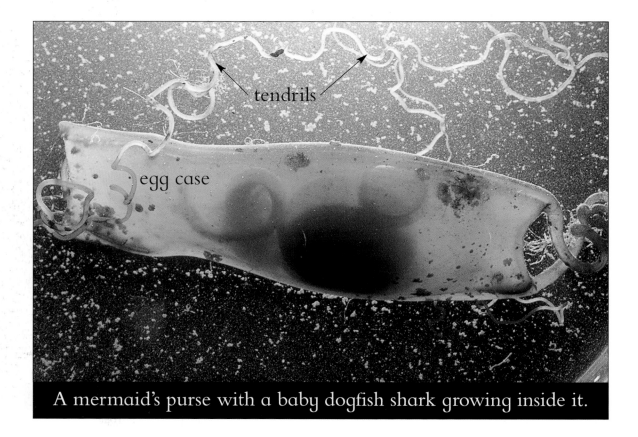

tendrils

egg case

A mermaid's purse with a baby dogfish shark growing inside it.

Baby sharks are called **pups**. This dogfish shark has just hatched from his egg case. As soon as he is born, he has to look after himself. Shark pups learn to stay away from adult sharks who may eat them.

This dogfish shark pup must learn to look after himself.

Unusual sharks

This basking shark catches plankton as it swims along.

This basking shark looks fierce, but it is not fierce at all. It swims slowly near the **surface** of the water with its mouth wide open to catch as much **plankton** as it can.

lobe

This wobbegong looks like a rock overgrown with seaweed.

Wobbegongs live near Australia. They lie very still on the sea bed and wait for octopus and crabs to pass by. Wobbegongs have a spotted pattern on them and **lobes** that stick out of their heads. This makes them hard to spot.

19

Sharks and people

Some people catch sharks for their oil and meat.

Some sharks are in danger. Basking sharks are hunted for their oily livers. The liver can be a quarter of its body weight. People eat the fins and meat of black-tip sharks. Like the great white shark, these sharks are becoming **rare**.

Some people enjoy watching sharks and even filming them. But they have to be careful not to get bitten. Some divers wear suits made of chain mail to stop a shark's teeth biting their skin.

This diver is filming sharks.

Shark facts

- Most sharks are less than 2 metres (6 feet) long. The smallest shark is only 25 cm (10 inches) long.

- A shark's skeleton is not made of bone, but **gristle**, rather like the tip of your nose.

- A shark's skin is very tough. It is covered in small, sharp, tooth-like scales.

A hammerhead shark is named after the shape of its head.

- Sharks have between two and over 100 **pups**. Pregnant females have their babies away from other sharks and where there is plenty of food.

Great white sharks can grow up to 12 metres.

- In some parts of the world, swimmers have been attacked by sharks. The great white shark is one of the most dangerous. But far more people are killed by cars than by sharks.

Glossary

coral   a hard ridge made by millions of tiny sea animals

gills   the slits at the side of a fish's head, used for breathing

gristle   a strong material that makes up a shark's skeleton

lobes   a wobbegong shark's lobes are small outgrowths of skin on its head

mermaid's purse   the egg case of a dogfish

plankton   tiny plants and animals in the sea

pup   a baby shark

rare   not many left

shallow   not deep

shoal   a big group of fish

surface   the top of something, in this case the sea

tendril   a thin line that clings to something stronger for support

Index